Featherstone

Series editor
ALISTAIR
BRYCE-CLEGG

# 50

## fantastic ideas for
# exploring food

JUDIT HORVATH

Featherstone
An imprint of Bloomsbury Publishing Plc

50 Bedford Square            1385 Broadway
London                       New York
WC1B 3DP                     NY 10018
UK                           USA

www.bloomsbury.com

Bloomsbury is a registered trademark of Bloomsbury Publishing Plc

First published 2017

British Library Cataloguing-in-Publication Data
A catalogue record for this book is available from the British Library.

ISBN:
PB 978-1-4729-2255-7
ePDF 978-1-4729-2477-3

Library of Congress Cataloging-in-Publication Data
A catalogue record for this book is available from the Library of Congress.

10 9 8 7 6 5 4 3 2 1

Printed and bound in India by Replika Press Pvt Ltd.

This book is produced using paper that is made from wood grown in managed, sustainable
forests. It is natural, renewable and recyclable. The logging and manufacturing processes
conform to the environmental regulations of the country of origin.

To view more of our titles please visit www.bloomsbury.com

# Contents

Introduction ...............................................4

## Physical development
Building a gingerbread house ...............6
Mud pie mixing.........................................8
Kneading bread ........................................9
Sowing, growing and gardening............10
Making biscuits .......................................11
Building a simple oven .........................12
Making fruity jam.....................................13

## Personal, social and emotional development
Family cookbook ...................................14
Creating your own menu .......................16
Toffee popcorn gift ................................17
Creating a pictorial shopping list...........18
Create your own sandwich....................19
Organising a birthday party .................20
Creating a herb blend............................22

## Communication and language
Secret message roll................................23
Going to market ......................................24
Little Red Hen puppet theatre ..............26
Giant pizza..............................................27
Organising a mud work station ............28
Food from different cultures..................29
The chef's library ...................................30

## Mathematics
Pasta size comparison ..........................31
Dishing up ..............................................32
Microwave biscuits.................................33
Measuring with scales: scones ............34
Pound cake ............................................35
Making potato wedges...........................36
Shortbread shape biscuits ...................37
Breakfast muffin making........................38

## Literacy
Personalised flapjacks...........................40
Bilingual smoothies ...............................41
Sign language recipe cards...................42
Rhymes and songs about food ............43
Gingerbread Man storyboard ...............44
Food shopping around the world..........46
Letter pretzels.........................................47

## Expressive arts and design
Sensory kitchen......................................48
Potion making for magic yoghurt ..........49
Bread sculpting ......................................50
Taste test: juice making.........................52
Texture cards .........................................53
Make your own apron.............................54
Kitchen utensil musical..........................55

## Understanding the world
Farm journey ..........................................56
Cookie swap party .................................57
Bread from different cultures.................58
Spices around the world .......................60
Harvest around the world......................61
Foraging trip ..........................................62
Video-recipe: cupcakes........................64

# Introduction

## The aims of the book

We know that young children learn most effectively when they are feeling well and having fun. Educational theory comes to life through children's play, and although its recognition has changed through the centuries, the essence and importance of early years education remain unchanged: young children's learning and development takes place through their engagement with the world around them. There are many ways in which children can learn alongside adults, and the most enjoyable and engaging ones can be found right on the adults' doorsteps, requiring no special organisation, cost or effort.

Making food together is an obvious choice of early years activity. Simple cooking tasks are mines of learning activities and all children, regardless of their age, stage or interest, can be involved in each step of the process. Following old traditions helps young children to understand their heritage and who they are in the world around them, and to see and understand similarities and differences. Reading recipes and making connection between print and speech helps children's literacy. Personal, social and emotional development is aided by listening to personal stories and memories while baking and sharing edible goods, and by accomplishing children's personal targets when taking responsibility for small tasks, such as chopping dried fruit or cutting out biscuits. Mathematical concepts are brought to life by measuring and weighing ingredients, counting baked products and planning proportions. Children will also recognise the passing time when – during waiting for the food to cook or bake – past events are being retold. While decorating or dishing up food, creative development gains a new meaning by exchanging paint for chocolate and jam. In this process, children communicate with other people, listen and pay attention, easily understand what is being said due to the real life demonstration and develop their vocabulary when making sense of various tasks. Their imagination is boosted when they re-experience the events in their Muck kitchen (page 28). Inevitably, involving children in all real everyday activities aids their holistic growth. The activities are simple enough for young children to complete with minimal adult guidance; therefore, the projects have the potential to result in a genuine sense of achievement for young children.

## The structure of the book

The structure of the book is based on the seven learning areas of the Early Years Foundation Stage, however, it fits different types and levels of curriculum as well. Each learning area has at least seven activities, providing a varied selection to suit different ages, stages and interests.

Each activity description contains a list of resources required (What you need). The activities are clearly explained step-by-step, with easy-to-follow instructions ('What to do'), and suggested extensions and variations for ensuring flexible provision to match different settings, children and individual needs. Additional ideas for similar activities are very helpful when there is a need to take the learning further or to change the direction of the activity. The activities also include some observation questions that offer brief suggestions on how to support the children's learning effectively and to enrich their learning in the future.

The section titled 'What's in it for the children?' describes the educational aims and learning opportunities of the activity. Where needed – due to specific hazards being involved in the flow of the activity – useful information is added in the 'Health & Safety' section, however, your usual Health & Safety procedures should always be followed. For some activities, therefore, adults need to accomplish certain tasks to ensure they are completed safely, e.g. handling sharp tools to cut hard fruit. Practitioners should make informed decisions about which tasks can be safely accomplished by which of their children, and adhere to the Health & Safety procedures in place within their setting.

## Learning through food

When loved, listened to and appreciated, children will be enthusiastic about learning. The more children learn the greater their confidence will grow, the more confident children are the more people they can unconditionally love, and when loved and listened to … this is the strong circle of success.

Children enter the world biologically programmed to want to learn and to learn quickly. Children are natural explorers, brilliant at collecting, gathering, sorting and, given the opportunity, making things from scratch. When they see, hear, smell, touch and taste, their brain is provided with an immense inventory of information which, through purposeful activities, develop into a cohesive relationship between mind and body.

Cooking satisfies and stimulates all domains of development – cognitive, social, emotional and physical – and it provides numerous opportunities for physical mind-body connections, resulting in engagement rather than work. Cooking with children is an activity that meets the needs of children at any age or stage, can be adjusted to the individual child, and will encourage children to grow up making healthy cooking their natural choice.

## Allergies

Before undertaking cookery activities with the children in your setting it is vital to ascertain any allergies or food intolerances so make sure parents and carers are invited to advise you of any restrictions to their child's diet.

The recipes featured in this book are simple, using everyday ingredients, and therefore the majority of them can be substituted to suit allergen-free diets. Eggs can be replaced by mixing a spoonful of vinegar into the choice of milk or milk-substitute and letting it stand for five minutes. One egg is about 50-60g, therefore, 50-60ml of liquid should be used in place. A wide range of gluten free flours are sold in shops and supermarkets, an obvious choice is the gluten-free blends, however you can use buckwheat, gram or rice flour. Dairy milk and butter can be replaced with coconut, soy or olive oil based products.

# Building a gingerbread house

## Physical development

## What you need:

- A gingerbread mixture
  - 350g flour
  - 1 tsp bicarbonate of soda
  - 2 tsp ground ginger
  - 1 tsp ground cinnamon
  - 125g butter
  - 175g light soft brown sugar
  - 1 egg
  - 4 tbsp golden syrup
- House templates cut from paper
  - Sidewall:
    2 rectangles 6 cm x 8 cm
  - Front/backwall:
    2 squares 6 cm x 6 cm
  - Gable walls front/back:
    2 triangles 5 cm x 5 cm x 6 cm
  - Roof:
    2 rectangles 6 cm x 10 cm
- Mixing bowl
- Knife
- Baking paper
- Wire cooling rack
- Baking tray
- Royal icing as glue
  - 2 egg whites
  - 500g icing sugar
- Piping bag and simple nozzle
- Flaked almonds
- Generous amounts of sweets

## What to do:

1. Make the gingerbread mixture by combining all of the ingredients, and once dough is smooth, set aside.

2. Preheat the oven to 180° C. Line two baking trays with greaseproof paper.

3. Roll the dough out to a 0.5 cm thickness on a lightly floured surface. Using the paper templates, cut out the gingerbread house shapes and place on the baking tray, leaving a gap between them. Select any unbroken flaked almonds and gently poke them into the roof sections, pointy-end first, to look like roof tiles

4. Bake for 12-15 minutes, or until lightly golden-brown. Leave on the tray for ten minutes and then move to a wire rack to finish cooling.

5. When cooled, decorate with the writing icing and cake decorations.

6. Put the egg whites in a large bowl, sift in the icing sugar, then stir to make a thick, smooth icing. Spoon into a piping bag with a medium nozzle.

7. Pipe generous snakes of icing along the wall edges, one by one, to join the walls together. Use a small bowl/sponges to support the walls from the inside, then allow to dry, ideally for a few hours.

8. Once dry, remove the supports and fix the roof panels on. The angle is steep so these may need to be held on firmly for a few minutes until the icing starts to dry. Dry completely, ideally overnight.

9. To decorate, pipe a little icing and add embellishments.

## Taking it forward

- Make themed buildings such as schools, castles, bridges etc.

## Observational questions

- How does the child control small movements?

- Can the child concentrate for long periods of time?

## What's in it for the children?

Children will develop hand-eye coordination and exercise their muscles, gaining fine motor control.

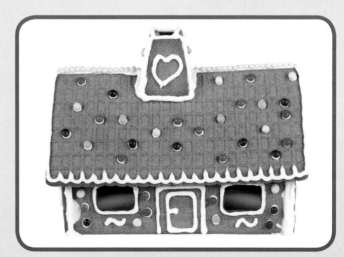

# Mud pie mixing
## Physical development

## What you need:

- Earth/soil
- Sand
- Pebbles
- Leaves
- Sticks
- Wooden spoons
- Small bowls and plastic containers
- Plastic and paper cups
- A variety of baking trays
- A play oven made of cardboard or a wooden crate
- Laminated recipe cards

## What to do:

1. Provide tools (various containers, trays and tins) and ingredients (earth, sand, pebbles, leaves).

2. Provide buckets of water or set up a play session near a tap/running water.

3. Encourage children to make mud pies by providing laminated (waterproof) pictorial recipe cards.

**Taking it forward**

- Set up a role play mud café.

**Observation questions**

- How does the child manipulate material?

- How does the child control tools? One-handed or two-handed? Does the child use mostly one hand? Which?

**What's in it for the children?**

Children will make connections between their movement and the marks they make. This enhances gross motor skills as the children handle materials and work around the mud station, carry full shovels of earth/sand or balance full pots of water, lift and pour containers, stir and scoop with utensils, squat, stand, sit and physically move around.

# Kneading bread
## Physical development

## What you need:

- Bread dough
  - 500g flour
  - 350g water
  - 5 tbsp olive oil
  - pinch of salt
  - 15g fresh yeast
- Mixing bowl
- Olive oil
- Baking tray

## What to do:

1. Make dough by combining all the ingredients in a large bowl.

2. Cover a flat, smooth surface lightly with oil and turn the dough onto it.

3. Cut into individual pieces for each child.

4. Model the kneading.

5. Make shapes as desired, and bake on 200° C. If the children made rolls bake for 15-20 minutes, if prepared as a loaf, bake for 45-50 minutes, until the loaf sounds hollow when tapped on the bottom.

**Taking it forward**
- Set up a role play bakery.
- Add flavours on themed days such as spices, herbs etc.

**Observation questions**
- How does the child control their own body?
- Does the child show a preference for a dominant hand?
- Can the child apply pressure?

**What's in it for the children?**

Children will build muscle control while strengthening hand-eye coordination. They will have the opportunity to make direct connections to food, including considering where it comes from, what physical shapes it takes and how it supports the human body.

50 fantastic ideas for exploring food

## What you need:

- Wheat seeds
- Garden tools such as a shovel and rake
- **Planting soil** (wheat grows in many types of soil, but it grows best in well-drained loam or clay-loam soils)
- **Very deep planting pots** (wheat needs 31 to 38 centimetres of water to produce a good crop)

## What to do:

1. Soak the seeds overnight in water then rinse before planting.

2. If planting in pots, fill pots with soil ¾ full and place some seeds on top. Cover with soil.

3. If planting outside (ideally in the spring), then prepare the soil by loosening it with a shovel and raking it smooth. Create raised lines, put seeds in and cover gently.

4. Water the seeds regularly and follow their growth.

**Taking it forward**

- Grow a range of different crops.

**Observational questions**

- Can the child control their large muscles to manipulate objects?

**What's in it for the children?**

Children will move freely, with pleasure and confidence in a range of ways, such as slithering, shuffling, walking, running, while controlling their own bodies and using strength to manipulate the environment.

# Making biscuits

## Physical development

## What you need:

- Biscuit dough:
  - 300g flour
  - 200g butter
  - 100g sugar
  - pinch of salt
  - 1 egg yolk
  - zest of one lemon
- Mixing bowl
- Flour to dust
- Variety of rolling pins (making different impressions)
- Variety of cutters

## What to do:

1. Make the biscuit dough by combining all the ingredients in a large bowl.

2. Rest it in the fridge for 30 minutes.

3. Cover a flat, smooth surface lightly with flour and turn the dough onto it.

4. Cut into individual pieces for each child.

5. Model the rolling and how to apply pressure.

6. Let the children experiment with different rolling pins. Cut shapes as desired, and bake on 180° C. Bake for 12-15 minutes, until golden yellow.

**Taking it forward**

- Organise a bake sale for charity.
- Add flavours on themed days, or host a traditional tea party.
- Eat the biscuits at snack time as a treat.

**Observation question**

- How do the children use their fingers? (Consider this in preparation for writing and fine motor skill development.)

**What's in it for the children?**

Children will build small muscle control, while experiencing how to control their own strengths. They will apply fine motor skills when using their fingers to cut biscuits.

# Building a simple oven

## Physical development

## What you need:

- Old bricks
- Plenty of sand and water
- Plenty of earth/clay
- Oven door made from old baking tray or saucepan
- Tarpaulin (2m x 2.5m) optional
- Sheets of wet newspaper

## What to do:

1. Create a bed of sand: dig a 10 cm deep hole in the ground and cover with a 10-15 cm thick layer of sand. Tamp and smooth into an even, level bed. For improved waterproofing lay a tarpaulin in the hole before filling up with sand.

2. Set oven bricks into the bed of sand to create the oven floor. For the door, use an old baking tray or old large saucepan (so you would cut out the door space accordingly).

3. Make a pile of bricks on the floor around the sand. Make the walls near vertical at first, to give your loaves 'head room'.

4. Mix mud/clay.

5. First, cover the sand with sheets of wet newspaper (so that later you know where the void ends and the oven begins). Smooth them down flat. Press handfuls of clay mix around the base of the sand form. Use your fingers as a gauge to guide in, maintaining thickness. Make a layer at least 7 cm thick. Cover with three layers of mud.

6. Cut out a doorway and remove the sand.

7. Fire-dry it.

8. To bake, fire the oven without a door cover. Then clean out the fire and load things to bake into the hot oven.

9. Use an old baking tray or saucepan for the over door. while baking.

### Taking it forward

- Children can prepare their own vegetables for baking (for example wrapping washed potatoes in aluminium foil).

### Observational questions

- Does the child show increasing strength?

### What's in it for the children?

Children will experience the effects of hard work/exercise on the human body. They will develop an understanding of the human mechanism (exercise-muscles-hunger-food).

# Making fruity jam
## Physical development

## What you need:

- **Plenty of fruit** (strawberries, plum, apples, apricots, damsons etc. see activity for measurements)
- **Jam sugar**
- **Lemons, almonds, rhubarb for flavour** (optional)
- **Jars for potting**

## What to do:

**1.** To make plum jam: 1.5kg plums, 1.5kg jam sugar, 650-700ml water. Wash the fruit and cut in halves, removing the stones. Put the water, kernels and plums into a pan, bring slowly to boiling point and simmer gently until the fruit is cooked and the liquid reduced. Add the sugar, stir until dissolved and bring to the boil. Boil briskly for about 10-15 minutes and test for jellying by placing some on a cold plate. Pot and cover the jam.

**2.** To make apricot jam: 450g dried apricots, 1300ml water, juice of 1 lemon, 1.5kg jam sugar, some shelled almonds (optional). Wash the apricots thoroughly, cover with the water and soak for 24 hours. Put the fruit into a pan with the water in which it was soaked, add the lemon juice and simmer for ½ hour, or until soft, stirring from time to time. Add the sugar and almonds, stir until the sugar has dissolved and boil rapidly until setting point is reached, stirring frequently, as the jam tends to stick. Pot and cover in the usual way.

**3.** To make damson jam: 1.75kg damsons, 2.7kg jam sugar, 650-700ml water. Wash the damsons, add the water, bring to the boil and simmer until the fruit is cooked. Add the sugar, stir until dissolved and bring to the boil. Boil quickly, removing the stones with a slotted spoon as they rise. After about ten minutes of boiling, test for setting. Pot and cover in the usual way.

**Taking it forward**
- Organise a fruit picking trip

**Observational questions**
- How does the child use tools?

**What's in it for the children?**

Children will experience using tools and the basic rules of self-care (considering health and safety).

### Health & Safety
Take great care handling boiling fruit and jam: very high temperatures are reached. Keep the children at a safe distance.

# Family cookbook

Personal, social and emotional development

## What you need:

- Eight pieces of paper
- One piece of card
- Family photographs
- Photocopies of family recipes
- Two sewing pins
- One coloured-tip pin
- One dull-tipped needle
- Velcro
- Length of linen thread
- Pencil
- Scissors
- Glue stick

## What to do:

1. Lay each piece of paper on a flat surface, match up the corners and fold, making a good crease for the spine. Then stack all eight sheets, spine on spine on spine. This creates one section for the text, called a signature.

2. With the card laying horizontally on a flat surface, lay the stacked signature on the left side with the spine (folded edge) to the right and the pages, edge to the left. There should be equal amounts of card showing to the top, bottom and sides of the signature. Make a small mark with a pencil right next to the spine at the bottom and the top. Remove the signature and fold the card on the marks. Make another good crease.

3. Neatly stack the signature on the coloured card, spine on spine. Clip things into place with the sewing pins. Use the pencil to mark three sewing points in the centre of the signature, one in the middle and one about an inch from the top edge and one about an inch from the bottom edge. Use pin to poke holes at the sewing points. Thread the needle with the linen thread. There should be one long thread tail and one short tail, not equal lengths. Start sewing in the centre hole in the middle of the book. For the final sewing step, put the needle and thread back through the centre hole. Once the two ends have been returned to the middle, one tail should be laid to the right, one tail to the left and the middle loop should be in the centre. Gently pull the two tails to pull the sewing taut. Proceed to tie a square knot. Trim the thread tails.

4. Stick the family photographs and recipes in and use in cooking activities.

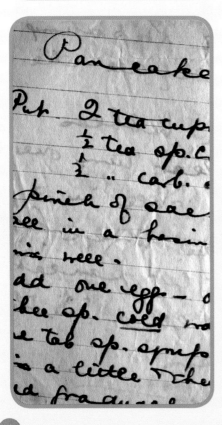

## Taking it forward

- Make a nursery cookbook dedicating a recipe for each child. Note children's own language when giving instructions.

## Observational questions

- Does the child understand that some things are theirs, some things are shared, and some things belong to other people?

- Does the child display a sense of pride?

## What's in it for the children?

When sharing the book children can explain their own knowledge and understanding and show interest in others.

# Creating your own menu

## Personal, social and emotional development

## What you need:

- Pieces of card/cardboard
- Decorating materials: pencil, scissors, glue stick
- Old/recycled cooking/recipe magazines and books

## What to do:

1. Create a cardboard menu about A4 size.
2. Make notes about children's favourite foods, encourage them to chose from their own pictures or cut images from magazines.
3. Create a menu for each child, writing their names next to them (or add their photograph).

### Taking it forward

- Cook children's chosen menu for dinner, and host an open dinner party for parents.
- Use the menus in a restaurant role play.
- Create pictorial recipe cards for chosen dishes.

### Observational questions

- Does the child take part in the social interaction?
- How does the child express their own views?

### What's in it for the children?

Children will be taking part and drawing others into social interaction.

# Toffee popcorn gift

Personal, social and emotional development

## What you need:

- Pieces of cardboard to make paper cones or brown paper bags
- For the corn:
  - 100g popping corn
  - 1 tbsp sunflower oil
  - 1 tsp butter
  - 1 pinch sea salt

or microwaveable popcorn

- For the toffee coating:
  - 40g soft brown sugar
  - 4 tbsp golden syrup or honey
  - 30g butter
  - 1 tsp water

## What to do:

1. Heat the oil in a large saucepan. Add the corn and swirl it around to coat it in the oil. Cover with a lid and leave over a low heat until all the popping has stopped, shaking the pan occasionally.

2. Meanwhile, add the butter, syrup, sugar and water to a saucepan over a medium-high heat. Stir constantly with a wooden spoon until the butter has melted and the sugar has dissolved. Bring to the boil and let it bubble rapidly for four to five minutes, stirring throughout, until the mixture is a dark, toffee colour.

3. Pour the toffee sauce over the popcorn, and stir to coat all the kernels. Leave to cool slightly and let the toffee sauce harden for around five minutes before serving.

4. During the cooling time create simple paper cones: Make a paper disk by cutting a circle out from any kind of soft paper. The height of the cone will be determined by the radius of the circle. Draw a triangle wedge by drawing two lines from the side of the circle to the centre of the circle, starting the lines 3-5 cm apart from each other. Cut the triangle wedge out of the circle. Bring the cut sides of the disc together. Tape the inside of the cone closed.

5. Fill up the cones with the cooled popcorn and enjoy.

### Taking it forward

- Experiment with different flavours by using herbs, spices, chocolate etc. to cover popcorn.

### Observational questions

- Can the child name his/her friends? Does the child display an understanding of friendship?

### What's in it for the children?

Children will gain an awareness of their own feelings, and understand that some actions and words can affect others' feelings, while accepting the needs of others by sharing resources, sometimes with support from others.

### ✚ Health & Safety

Take great care when heating hot oil in the presence of children. Warn them to stay well back while an adult is using it.

# Create a pictorial shopping list

Personal, social and emotional development

## What you need:

- Pieces of card/cardboard
- Decorating materials: pencil, scissors, glue stick
- Old/recycled cooking/recipe magazines, books, store leaflets

## What to do:

1. Create a board from card, about A4 size.

2. Working in a small group make notes about each child's favourite food items and talk about shopping with their family.

3. Encourage the children to make a shopping list by cutting out pictures of food items from leaflets and magazines.

4. Invite them to write the name of their favourite food items next to the pictures.

5. Take children to a local store to buy everyday staple food, such as bread and milk.

Taking it forward

- Visit the local market.
- Use shopping in role play.

Observational questions

- Does the child show an understanding of pretend play?

What's in it for the children?

Role play provides plenty of opportunities for social interaction and communication.

# Create your own sandwich
Personal, social and emotional development

## What you need:

- **Bread** (e.g. white bread, brown bread, roll, wrap, pitta bread, English muffins)
- **Cold cuts of meat** (salami, ham, turkey, chicken, etc.)
- **Assortment of cheese** (Swiss, cheddar, etc.)
- **Garnish** (lettuce, tomatoes, pickles, olives, carrots, cucumbers, etc.)
- **Condiments** (ketchup, mustard, mayonnaise, salad dressing)
- **Paper plates**
- **Serviettes**
- **Tongs, forks**
- **Butter and knife** (if age-appropriate)

## What to do:

1. Gather all of the various sandwich ingredients. Put different groups of ingredients on separate trays.
2. Give each child a paper plate and encourage them to create their own sandwich, using whatever ingredients they wish to use. Encourage them to select their sandwich ingredients using plastic tongs.
3. After each child has created their sandwich, let them enjoy eating it.
4. Create a variety of closed and open sandwiches.

### Taking it forward

- Take photographs of the finished sandwiches and create a sandwich menu.
- Visit a local sandwich bar or shop as field research.

### Observational questions

- Does the child make choices?

### What's in it for the children?

Children will learn about cultures, tastes, nutrition and developing healthy eating habits. They also learn about making choices, while using fine motor skills when holding utensils and selecting ingredients.

### Health & Safety

Bear in mind any food allergies or intolerances and oversee the children's choices as they assemble their sandwiches.

# Organising a birthday party

Personal, social and emotional development

## What you need:

- Birthday cake
  - rotary hand mixer
  - large mixing bowl
  - a baking tin (20-25cm)
  - wire cooling rack
  - 225g butter (softened, plus extra for greasing)
  - 350g caster sugar
  - 1 tbsp vanilla extract
  - 5 large egg whites
  - 325g plain flour
  - 25g cornflour
  - 1½ tbsp baking powder
  - 250ml buttermilk
- Chocolate sprinkles
- Icing sugar
- Balloons
- Confetti
- Coloured cards
- Triangle template
- Scissors
- Sticky tape
- Ribbon
- Choice of musical CDs

## What to do:

1. Bake a cake: Beat the butter and sugar in a large bowl until light and fluffy. Add the vanilla extract and the egg whites, a little at a time. Mix together the flour, cornflour and baking powder. Add the dry ingredients in three batches, alternating with the milk. Pour the mixture into a lined baking tin and bake at 180° C for 30 minutes or until a skewer inserted into the middle comes out clean. Allow the cake to rest in the tin for ten minutes, then turn it out onto a wire rack. Cool completely, then decorate with icing sugar and sprinkles.

2. Ask the children to create some personalised paper bunting: using a template, draw the triangles onto coloured paper/card, marking the position of the holes. Cut triangles and make holes with a hole puncher. Cut a length of ribbon or string. Tie a loop on one end. From the opposite end to the loop carefully (so as not to tear the paper) thread on triangles one by one. With the right side of the paper facing you, thread the ribbon/string through the right hand hole from the back to the front, then thread it through the second hole from the front to the back. Once all triangles are on, create a loop on the other end. Decorate the triangles with pictures of the birthday boy or girl.

3. Decorate a room or dedicated party area, choosing a child to supervise the decoration. Choose music with the celebrated person in mind.

- Organise a themed tea party.

Observational questions

- Does the child name friends?
- Can the child describe the positive qualities of others?

What's in it for the children?

Children will learn to understand that their own actions affect other people, and become aware of behavioural expectations in a given environment.

50 fantastic ideas for exploring food

# Creating a herb blend

Personal, social and emotional development

## What you need:

- **Fresh herbs** (basil, parsley, coriander, rosemary, lavender etc.)
- **Sea salt**
- **Baking sheet/cookie sheet**
- **Paper bags, both large and small**
- **String**

## What to do:

1. Buy a selection of fresh herbs.

2. To air-dry: gather five to ten sprigs and tie them with string or a rubber band. The smaller the bundle, the easier and faster they will dry. Put the bundle of herbs, stem-side up, in a paper bag. Tie the end of the bag closed, being sure not to crush the herbs, and poke a few holes in the bag for ventilation. Hang the bag by the stem end in a warm, well-ventilated room for about one week.

3. To oven-dry: place herb leaves or seeds on a baking tray one inch deep or less. Put herbs in the oven on a very low heat for two to four hours. To see if the herbs are dry, check if the leaves crumble easily. Oven-dried herbs will cook a little, removing some of the potency and flavour.

4. Ask the children to crumble the leaves, then smell, choose and mix them.

5. Place the mixtures into little bags, marked with the children's photographs so they know who made which.

### Taking it forward

- Forage herbs.
- Buy herbs from a market with the children.
- Make herb bread or scones.

### Observational questions

- Does the child express their own likes and dislikes?
- Can the child describe and reason their own choices?

### What's in it for the children?

Children will learn about themselves and others, they will learn that people's views differ. Children will practise expressing their opinion, and understand that their opinion is being listened to.

50 fantastic ideas for exploring food

# Secret message roll
## Communication and language

## What you need:

- Bread roll dough
  - 500g strong white bread flour, plus extra for dusting
  - 1 tsp salt
  - 2 tsp dried yeast
  - 30g butter
  - 100ml warm milk
  - 200ml warm water
  - semolina or porridge oats for dusting
- Large mixing bowl
- Tea towel
- Baking sheet lined with baking paper
- Aluminium foil
- Parchment paper
- Cling film
- Black marker or pencil

## What to do:

1. Make the bread roll dough by combining all the ingredients in a large bowl, then set aside to rest and rise, covered with a tea towel.

2. Meanwhile, cut up the parchment paper into small pieces and ask the children to draw/write/mark secret messages to their friends on the paper.

3. Take pieces of aluminium foil and wrap them around the parchment paper message, sealing with several folds.

4. Separate the mixture into equal parts (the ingredients make about ten rolls) and roll each part into a ball. Flatten each slightly with the palm of the hand and transfer the rolls to a baking tray, placing a message underneath (slightly press with fingers). Cover the tray with cling film and set aside for 30 minutes. Meanwhile, preheat the oven to 220° C. When the rolls have expanded, dust them with semolina/oats and transfer them to the oven. Bake for about 12-15 minutes, or until golden-brown and cooked through.

### Taking it forward
- Make fortune cookies to learn about different cultures.

### Observation questions
- Is the child interested in mark making?
- What is the child's preferred way to make marks?

### What's in it for the children?
Children will learn to follow simple instructions. They will experience that marks carry meaning, and the meaning can be interpreted in different ways by different people.

# Going to Market

## What you need:

- A selection of real vegetables: potatoes, peppers, cucumbers, an onion – as basics for cooking
- A selection of real fruit: tomatoes, as well as apples, pears, oranges, lemons are the most popular
- Selection of herbs
- Scales
- Paper or blackboards
- Pen or crayons
- Real penny coins
- Paper bags, both large and small
- String
- Tables
- Soft brown paper or construction paper
- Cardboard boxes (optional)
- Different coloured fabric as dressing-up clothes (scarves, t-shirts etc.)
- Oil, frying pan
- 2 tbsp honey
- 1 cup of orange juice

## What to do:

1. Set up three or four small tables in a row. Cover them with brown paper.
2. Ask the children to choose who they would like to be, buyer or seller, and encourage them to dress up.
3. Place cardboard boxes of food items on the tables, organise and ask children to set their prices, using store leaflets.
4. Ask 'buyers' what they would like to buy and encourage them to role play.
5. Once they have made their choices, gather children and clean and peel their goods.
6. Make a simple vegetable stew: heat the oil in a large pan, add the onion and fry slowly for five minutes. Add the other vegetables, cover and fry over a medium heat for five minutes, so they start to soften. Pour in the water and tomatoes, bring to the boil, cover and simmer for ten minutes, until the vegetables are tender. Sprinkle with the chopped parsley.
7. Make a simple fruit salad by peeling and cutting up fruit, and mix with honey and orange juice.

50 fantastic ideas for exploring food

**Taking it forward**

■ Host a dinner party.

■ Visit a local food market.

**Observational questions**

■ Can/do the children act according to their role and start conversations, such as 'How much does this potato cost?' etc.?

■ Can the child adapt their behaviour?

■ Does the child show interest in new situations?

**What's in it for the children?**

Children will begin to be able to negotiate and solve problems including sharing, giving, or dealing with incidents where someone has taken their possession.

50 fantastic ideas for exploring food

# Little Red Hen puppet theatre

## Communication and language

## What you need:

- Little Red Hen storybook
- A big cardboard box
- Two tea towels
- Masking tape
- Scissors
- Paint, tinsel, fairy lights (optional)
- Paper
- Drawing tools: pen, pencil, crayon etc.
- Ironing board, tablecloth
- Portable music player
- Some CDs of favourite songs

## What to do:

1. To make the theatre: cut out the base and back panel of the box so you have a stand-alone stage frame: one long side and two short sides as flaps to keep it upright. Out of the long side, cut a proscenium arch (the frame of a stage) leaving about 10cm around the sides and top. There should be no bottom edge, just a square opening like an archway. The two side panels should allow the proscenium arch to stand up by itself. Attach curtains to the backstage side of the arch by using two tea towels. Use masking tape or a large stapler to stick them into place. Prop the puppet theatre on a dining table to put on a show. Decorate as required.

2. To make simple puppets: draw the characters from the story of *The Little Red Hen*, cut around each picture and tape lollipop sticks to the back of each.

3. To make the puppet stage: put the tablecloth over the ironing board to conceal what is going on backstage. A well-organised backstage makes for a better show, so organise the puppets and props in the order that they will be needed. Put props in one box and puppets in another.

4. Read the story aloud while children act out the narrative with the puppets.

5. Play songs to start and finish, and during puppet changeovers.

## Taking it forward

- Organise a puppet show for children to share.
- Make simple bread rolls to share at the end of story.

## Observation questions

- Can the child recognise familiar sounds? For example the voices of their friends, animal sounds etc.
- Can the child memorise the storyline or short sentences?

## What's in it for the children?

Children will listen to stories with increasing attention and recall, while joining in with repeated refrains and anticipating key events and phrases in rhymes and stories.

# Giant Pizza

## Communication and language

### What you need:

- Pizza dough
  - 300g strong white bread flour (plus extra for dusting)
  - 1 tsp salt
  - 7g instant yeast
  - 200ml warm water
  - 2 tbsp olive oil
- Baking sheet lined with baking paper
- Selection of pizza toppings: cold cuts of meat (ham, salami, chicken), cheese, tomato sauce, green and black olives, vegetables (sweetcorn, pepper, tomato), herbs
- Large mixing bowl
- Tea towel
- Paper and pencils
- Paper plates
- Serviettes
- Large blanket

### What to do:

1. Make the pizza dough by combining all the ingredients in a large bowl, then set aside to rest and rise, covered with a tea towel.

2. Prepare pizza toppings, and design the pizza with the children, make drawings, clearly indicating 'what goes where'.

3. On a floured surface, roll out the dough into large discs, using a rolling pin. The dough needs to be very thin as it will rise in the oven. Lift the discs onto two floured baking sheets.

4. Heat the oven to 220° C. Smooth some sauce over the bases with the back of a spoon. Scatter with chosen toppings, drizzle with olive oil and season. Put each pizza, still on the baking sheet, on top of the preheated tray. Bake for ten to 15 minutes until crisp.

5. Once baked, compare the result to the children's drawings.

6. Sit the group of children on a large blanket and consume pizza in a 'tear and share' fashion.

### Taking it forward

- Make a giant cookie to share.
- Visit a pizza shop or look through pizza menus.
- Create a pictorial recipe card.

### Observation questions

- Is the child able to negotiate and listen to others?
- Can the child follow simple instructions?

### What's in it for the children?

Children will learn to express their views and negotiate with others. They will gain experience in being listened to and listening to others, while focusing on particular events.

# Organising a mud work station
## Communication and language

## What you need:

- Sand
- Earth
- Leaves, bits of plants
- Empty containers, tins, bowls
- Paper bags
- Wooden spoons
- Plastic cups
- Pebbles/leaves/small shells to use as prop money
- Tables
- Old tyres

## What to do:

1. Organise space to provide different set-ups for the children to chose from: mud shop, mud café or a mud kitchen.

2. Ask children to create their own design.

3. Encourage mudlarking (scavenging for items of any value), digging in the soil to find interesting objects that stimulate discussions.

4. Set different scenarios:

   - Hand the children an object to transform: pretend they are cakes/biscuits etc. in order to develop pretence and their capacity to use their imaginations through mental representation.

   - Ask the children to become certain characters through symbolic actions, taking roles through choice and under direction in order to cooperate in play in different scenarios.

   - Set a problem to solve: how to make a cake, so children can negotiate and improvise via development and use of receptive and expressive language in interactive dialogue.

**Taking it forward**

- Organise a 'Clean mud kitchen' indoors, using flour, sugar and salt instead of soil.

**Observation questions**

- Can the child understand the use of objects (e.g. 'What do we use to cut things?')

- Does the child show understanding of prepositions such as 'under', 'on top', 'behind' when carrying out an action?

- Does the child respond to simple instructions, e.g. to get out or put away an object?

**What's in it for the children?**

Children will have opportunities to express themselves creatively, solve problems and play cooperatively while developing a growing affection for the planet Earth.

# Food from different cultures

Communication and language

## What you need:

- Recipe books representing different cultures
- Selection of food items from different countries, such as teas, fruits, breads, cold cuts, cheese
- Small bowls
- Scarf
- Cotton ball
- Vanilla extract

## What to do:

1. Source magazines and or cookbooks with recipes in.
2. Provide food items from different countries such as Spanish sausages, German salami, French bread, Italian tomato sauce, Belgian chocolate, Indian spiced tea, Chinese rice snacks.
3. Blind-fold children one at a time and encourage them to blind taste and then try to describe their experience.
4. Drop some vanilla extract on the cotton ball and hold under the children's nose while they are chewing.
5. Discuss the changes.

### Taking it forward

- The activity can be adjusted to suit different age groups if food items are pureed.
- Organise themed testing days such as 'Vegetables around the world', 'The world of bread' and so on.

### Observation questions

- Does the child use different ways to express opinion such as body language, mimicking, sounds etc.?

### What's in it for the children?

Children will have opportunities to express their own views about new experiences.

# The chef's library
## Communication and language

## What you need:

- Recipe books from the library or from home
- Selection of food related magazines
- Paper
- Pen
- Scissors
- Tables
- Chairs
- Clipboards

## What to do:

1. Organise a trip to the local library and borrow cookbooks.
2. Buy magazines with recipes in.
3. Provide art materials and help children to create their own personalised library card.
4. Set up a corner with a couple of tables/a small shelf for the books, magazines, and a table, chair, paper and a pen for the librarian.
5. Add some simple labels to the shelves/table, describing the types of books.
6. Add some signs above to create some opportunities for discussion.
7. On the librarian's table, place some mini clipboards with index cards attached, along with some writing pens. On some of the cards add some example writing such as 'please return by' and 'date borrowed' etc.
8. Encourage children to role play.

### Taking it forward
- Have books available that children can take home and return, so they can share their borrowed book in their home.
- Organise a book swap, where children can bring in their unwanted books and swap them with their friends.

### Observation questions
- Does the child engage in role play? What role does the child play?
- Is the child interested in books? Can the child indicate their favourite book?

### What's in it for the children?
Children will have opportunities for observing print in the environment and its direct link to speech and communication.

# Pasta size comparison

Mathematics

## What you need:

- Pasta dough
  - 125g flour
  - 1 egg
  - 2 tbsp water
  - ½ tsp salt
- Rolling pin
- Knife
- Bags of different types of pasta: spaghetti, farfelle, alphabet pasta, egg noodles, macaroni, lasagne, linguine, penne, tagliatelle
- Scales

## What to do:

1. Provide a selection of pasta.
2. Weigh the different types of pasta, study the difference in texture, feel, weight and appearance and let the children explore the different types.
3. Line different types in a row, by size.
4. Make your own pasta: in a medium sized bowl, combine flour and salt. Make a well in the flour, add the slightly beaten egg, and mix. The mixture should form a stiff dough. If needed, stir in 1 to 2 tablespoons of water. On a lightly floured surface, knead the dough for about three to four minutes. Roll the dough out to the desired thinness with a rolling pin. Use a knife to cut into strips of desired width.
5. Talk about how pasta is made and cooked.
6. Ask the children to estimate how long each type would take to cook.

## Taking it forward

- Make a simple pasta dish by adding tomato sauce, cheese and fresh basil, estimating the amount needed to cater for your group.

## Observation questions

- Does the child pay attention to details?
- Can the child recognise similarities and differences?

## What's in it for the children?

Children will develop an ability to group objects, they will practise comparing groups of objects and realise that things can be counted.

# Dishing Up

Mathematics

## What you need:

- Snack items, such as biscuits, rice cakes, pretzels, apples, apricots, raisins
- Small paper plates
- Tongs, serving spoons
- Serviettes
- A pen

## What to do:

1. Give children paper plates and ask them to draw the amount of food on it that they would like to eat.
2. Provide snack items on large trays.
3. Provide small plates and a variety of serving tools.
4. Ask children to serve up portions for their friends/carers/smaller-older siblings, based on how much they think they would eat.
5. Discuss the experience and share the food.

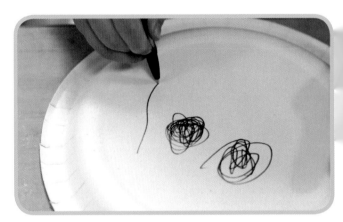

### Taking it forward

- Pour out drinks, estimating fluid quantities.

### Observation questions

- Does the child show an interest in solving simple problems?
- Does the child understand basic mathematical language such as bigger, smaller, more, less?

### What's in it for the children?

Children will develop an ability to guess and estimate, while beginning to identify mathematical problems based on their own interests and fascinations. They will make simple symbols and marks to represent the ideas of numbers and quantities.

# microwave biscuits

## What you need:

- Biscuit ingredients
  - 1 tbsp butter
  - 2 tbsp sugar
  - ¼ teaspoon vanilla or grated zest of lemon
  - 1 pinch salt
  - 1 egg yolk
  - 3 tbsp flour
- Sprinkles (optional)
- Tablespoon
- Teaspoon
- Microwaveable mugs
- Microwave oven

## What to do:

1. Give each child a mug, a tablespoon and a teaspoon, so they can measure their ingredients and make their biscuits individually.

2. Grease a microwave safe mug with vegetable oil.

3. Place butter in the mug and melt in the microwave (about 30 seconds).

4. Add sugar, vanilla or lemon zest and salt and stir together.

5. Add the egg yolk, mixing thoroughly.

6. Add flour and stir until combined.

7. Top with sprinkles and cook in the microwave for about 40-45 seconds. Check with a toothpick whether it is done.

8. Once ready, top with sprinkles if so desired.

### Taking it forward

- Make a simple fruit juice cocktail, adding ingredients with spoons.

### Observation questions

- Does the child show an interest in numbers?

- Does the child use numbers in their communication?

### What's in it for the children?

Children will develop an ability to estimate, while beginning to identify mathematical problems based on their own interests and fascinations.

# Measuring with scales: scones
## Mathematics

## What you need:

- Scone ingredients
  - 225g self raising flour
  - pinch of salt
  - 55g butter
  - 25g caster sugar
  - 150ml milk
  - milk to glaze
- Round cutter
- Electric scale
- Baking sheet, lined with baking parchment

## What to do:

1. Source all the ingredients and provide them separately for the children, indicating with a label what quantities they need of each (for the children to copy the numbers).

2. Ask the children to measure out the ingredients.

3. Heat the oven to 220° C.

4. Mix together the flour and salt and rub in the butter.

5. Stir in the sugar and then the milk to get a soft dough.

6. Turn on to a floured work surface and knead very lightly. Pat out to about 2cm thick. Use a round cutter to stamp out scones and place on a baking sheet. Lightly knead together the rest of the dough and stamp out more scones to use it all up.

7. Brush the tops of the scones with the beaten egg. Bake for 12-15 minutes until well-risen and golden.

### Taking it forward

- Use an old-fashioned scale with weights to further aid the children's understanding of quantity.
- Let children do the measuring themselves.

### Observation questions

- Does the child notice numerals in the environment?
- Can the child understand that things can be counted, weighed or measured?

### What's in it for the children?

Children will be able to recite number and recognise numeral significance.

# Pound cake

Mathematics

## What you need:

- Cake batter ingredients
  - 225g butter
  - 225g caster sugar
  - 4 eggs
  - 225g flour
  - finely grated zest of an orange
- Old fashioned scales
- A small rectangular cake tin
- A small round cake tin
- Wire cooling rack
- A balloon

## What to do:

1. Set an old fashioned scale to ½ pound or mark 225g on an analogue scales.

2. Explain to the children the difference between size and weight, and demonstrate by showing a large balloon and a bag of flour.

3. Weigh out the ingredients whilst explaining what pound cake means. 'Pound cake' refers to a type of cake traditionally made with a pound of each of four ingredients: flour, butter, eggs, and sugar. However, any cake made with a 1:1:1:1 ratio, by weight, of flour, butter, eggs, and sugar may also be called a pound cake, as it yields the same results.

4. Preheat the oven to 180°C. Grease the baking tins and line the base with two crossing, long strips of baking paper.

5. Beat the butter and sugar together until soft and creamy. Beat in the eggs one at a time, whisking well between each addition. Sift the flour into a bowl, add the orange zest and mix. Spoon the mixture into the tins and spread them level with the back of a spoon. Bake for about 30 minutes until golden and just firm to the touch. A skewer inserted into the centre should come out clean.

6. Cool in the tin for ten minutes then remove from the tin and leave to cool on a wire rack. Mix the icing sugar with a little water (about 2 tsp) to make a thin icing. Spread the icing over the top of the cake.

### Taking it forward

- Experiment with weight by comparing single items, such as one egg, one spoonful of sugar, one cube of butter, one potato, one apple etc.

### Observation questions

- Does the child estimate and then check by counting, measuring, weighing?

- Does the child compare groups, characteristics?

### What's in it for the children?

Children will be able to match numerals and quantity correctly, while showing curiosity about numbers by offering comments and asking questions.

# Making potato wedges

Mathematics

## What you need:

- Paper
- Dinner plate
- Coloured pencils
- Clipboards
- Baking potatoes
- Olive oil
- Seasoning: paprika, garlic salt, mixed herbs
- Baking tray

## What to do:

1. Ask each of the children to draw a plate on a sheet of paper, using a real plate as a template. Invite them to draw the number of wedges they think they could/would eat on their drawn plate.

2. Ask children to estimate how many potato wedges would equal to the amount they just drew.

3. Count how many children are in the group and estimate the number of wedges needed.

4. Involve the children in cleaning and cutting up the potatoes (they can be either peeled or not). Cut the potatoes in half and cut the halves into wedges, then count the number of wedges they made.

5. Cook the wedges: pre-heat the oven to about 200° C. Sprinkle some of the seasoning into a bowl and dip the potato wedges in, coating them lightly. Then, place them on the baking tray and drizzle lightly with the oil. Bake for about 30-40 minutes or until brown and crispy on the outside and tender in the middle.

6. Share out the wedges during an afternoon picnic.

### Taking it forward

- Estimate drinks needed with plastic cups, jugs and squash to experience relation between numbers and liquid quantities.

### Observation questions

- Does the child show enthusiasm when solving the problem?

- Does the child initiate/take part in discussion about mathematical problem?

### What's in it for the children?

Children will be able to apply number knowledge to practical, everyday situations in order to solve simple problems.

50 fantastic ideas for exploring food

# Shortbread shape biscuits
Mathematics

## What you need:

- Paper
- Scissors
- Biscuit ingredients
  - 125g butter
  - 55g caster sugar (plus extra to finish)
  - 180g plain flour
  - lavender or vanilla extract
- Knife
- Spatula
- Baking tray
- Wire cooling rack

## What to do:

1. Ask each of the children to draw shapes on a piece of paper and cut them out. Encourage children to draw a range of shapes.

2. Make the biscuits: beat the butter and the sugar together until smooth. Stir in the flour and chosen flavouring, making a smooth paste. Turn on to a work surface and gently pat with hands until the paste is 1 cm thick. Cut into shapes using children's templates and place on a baking tray with spatula. Sprinkle with caster sugar and chill in the fridge for 20 minutes. Heat the oven to 190° C. Bake in the oven for 15-20 minutes, or until pale golden-brown. Set aside to cool on a wire rack.

3. Discuss the shapes and try to find matching shapes in the environment.

## Taking it forward

- Prepare savoury shortbread by combining 150g plain flour, 75g grated parmesan, 100g soft unsalted butter and 1 large egg yolk. Roll the dough into a long cylinder shape and chill before cutting into thick discs to bake at 180°C for 15-20 mins.

## Observation questions

- Does the child show awareness of similarities of shapes in the environment?

## What's in it for the children?

Children will develop an interest in shape and space by playing with shapes or making arrangements with objects.

# Breakfast muffin making

## What you need:

- Dried cherries
- Raisins
- Dried apricots
- Pumpkin seeds
- Muffin ingredients to make 12
  - 2 large eggs
  - 150ml yogurt
  - 50ml oil
  - 100g apple, pureed
  - a banana
  - 4 tbsp honey
  - 200g wholemeal flour
  - 50g rolled oats (plus extra for sprinkling)
  - 1½ tsp baking powder
  - 1½ tsp bicarbonate of soda
  - 1½ tsp mixed spice
  - 100g dried fruit
  - 2 tbsp pumpkin seeds
- Large mixing bowl
- Spoon
- Jug
- Muffin tray
- Muffin cases
- Wire cooling rack

## What to do:

1. Mix the dried fruit and seeds in a large bowl. Provide small bowls for children to group/separate the fruits and seeds. While sorting, discuss the qualities using mathematical language such as small, big, more, less, circle, round, long etc.

2. Make the muffins: heat oven to 180° C. Line a 12-hole muffin tray with 12 large muffin cases. In a jug, mix the eggs, yogurt, oil, apple puree, banana, and honey. Tip the remaining ingredients into a large bowl, add a pinch of salt and mix to combine. Pour the wet ingredients into the dry ones then mix briefly (don't over mix as this will make the muffins heavy). Spoon the batter between the cases. Sprinkle the muffins with the oats and seeds. Bake for 25-30 minutes until golden and well risen, and a skewer inserted to the centre of a muffin comes out clean. Remove from the oven, transfer to a wire rack and leave to cool.

3. Share and enjoy.

## Taking it forward

- Give children sunflower and pumpkin seeds mixed in a bowl. Ask them to sort the seeds, separating the sunflower and pumpkin seeds. Prepare the seeds for roasting: spread the seeds in a single layer on a lined baking sheet and roast for 20 minutes to dry them out before adding the spices.

## Observation questions

- Does the child talk about quantities and qualities of objects?

## What's in it for the children?

Children will develop an interest in shape by talking about shapes or arrangements and by using shapes appropriately for tasks.

# Personalised flapjack

## What you need:

- White paper (A4)
- Pencil with eraser
- Markers
- Flapjack ingredients
  - 110g butter
  - 40g sugar
  - 2-3 tablespoons golden syrup
  - 175g porridge oats
  - optional ingredients: coconut flakes, sultanas, raisins, seeds
- Saucepan
- Spoon
- Lined baking tray

## What to do:

1. Ask children to select the optional ingredients they want to add to their personalised flapjack.

2. Make the flapjack: preheat the oven to 180° C. Line the tray with baking paper. Put the butter, sugar and golden syrup into a saucepan on a low heat and mix until it has melted and the sugar has dissolved. Take it off the heat and add the porridge and the extra ingredients if wanted. Mix well until the oats are coated. Pour the mixture into the tray. Flatten down with the back of a spoon. Place the flapjack in the oven for 10-20 minutes until golden brown on the top. Cut into shapes: squares, triangles, rectangles.

3. To make the recipe cards: break the recipe down into the easiest and shortest wording possible. Number the cards and write each step on the bottom of each piece of card in pencil with large letters. Ask children to trace back over the words with markers. Colour and decorate, then laminate if so desired.

## Taking it forward

- Can the child hear sounds in words?
- Does the child show interest in print/ books?

## Observation questions

- Look at various recipes and encourage the children to create their own recipe cards.
- For younger ages: read out a recipe and point to pictures of the ingredients in a food shop leaflet.

## What's in it for the children?

Children will understand the connection between print and words and know that they have a meaning.

# Bilingual smoothies

Literacy

## What you need:

- White paper (A4)
- Pencil with eraser
- Markers
- Smoothie ingredients
  - 1 banana
  - 1 mango
  - 500ml orange juice
  - 4 ice cubes
  - optional additions: coconut flakes, mint leaves, dried papaya etc.
- Liquidiser or smoothie maker

### Taking it forward

- Use a recipe/taste and language from the same culture, for example strawberry and custard smoothie (use strawberries instead of mango, banana and add runny custard instead of orange juice) – English; cinnamon and apple – Germany; damson and cloves etc.)

### Observation questions

- Does the child notice different sounds in different languages?
- Does the child show interest/ ask questions in the different languages?

### What's in it for the children?

Children will hear different sounds and understand that information can be relayed in writing and that print carries meaning and, in English, is read from left to right and top to bottom.

## What to do:

1. Ask children to select the extra ingredients they want to add to their personalised smoothie.

2. Make the smoothie: cut the mango down either side of the flat stone, then peel and cut the flesh into chunks. Peel and chop the banana. Put all the ingredients into a food processor or blender, then process until smooth and thick.

3. Make bilingual recipe cards (double sided cards with the English language steps on one side and with a related foreign instruction word or picture on the other).

   - Break the recipe down to the easiest and shortest wording possible.
   - Cut out as many card rectangles as there are steps in the recipe.
   - Number the cards so the steps will be easy to follow later.
   - Write each recipe instruction step on a piece of card in pencil.
   - On the other side, write an instruction word in a foreign language related to the recipe instruction step in pencil.
   - Ask children to trace back over the words with markers.
   - Colour and decorate, then laminate if so desired.

4. Discuss how different the words look and sound in different languages.

# Sign language recipe cards

Literacy

## What you need:

- White paper (A4)
- Pencil with eraser
- Markers
- Pictures of Makaton signs (or other sign language symbols)
- Cookie ingredients
  - 125g butter
  - 100g light brown soft sugar
  - 125g sugar
  - 1 egg
  - 1 tsp vanilla extract
  - 200g self-raising flour
  - 40g cocoa powder
  - ½ tsp salt
- Large mixing bowl
- Spoon
- Sieve
- Cookie tray
- Wire cooling rack

## What to do:

1. Make cookies: preheat the oven to 180°C. Cream the butter and sugar, then add the egg and vanilla extract. Sift in the flour and salt, then add the cocoa. Roll into walnut size balls. Place on an ungreased cookie sheet/baking paper. Cook for ten minutes until just golden round the edges. Take out of the oven and leave to harden for a minute before transferring to a wire cooling rack.

2. To make the sign language recipe cards:
   - Break the recipe down to the easiest and shortest wording possible.
   - Cut out as many card rectangles as there are steps in the recipe.
   - Number the cards so the steps will be easy to follow later.
   - Write each recipe instruction step on a piece of card in pencil.
   - On the other side, write picture (to refer to the sign language sign) related to the recipe instruction step in pencil.
   - Ask children to trace back over the drawing with markers.
   - Colour and decorate, then laminate if so desired.

### Taking it forward

- Watch TV cooking programmes with signing included.

### Observation questions

- Can child link sound to letter or image?
- Is the child interested in signs/symbols? Does the child ask questions?

### What's in it for the children?

Children will understand the differences between various symbolic systems, and they will experience that a picture, a spoken word and a sequence of letters can mean the same.

# Rhymes and songs about food

Literacy

## What you need:

- White paper
- Markers
- Coloured pencils
- Scissors
- Glue stick
- Cardboard
- Book of Nursery Rhymes
- Tray
- Cover for the tray

## What to do:

1. Ask children to listen to nursery rhymes/songs related to food: *Five currant buns, Hot cross bun, Sing a song of sixpence, Pat-a-cake, Simple Simon, Five fat sausages, I'm a little teapot, Jack Sprat.*

2. Ask children to draw the food item related to each rhyme/song. Cut out the pictures and stick them on card.

3. Use the cards in games such as Kim's game: place the pictures around a tray so that they are all visible. Tell children to take a look and invite them to review the pictures for a short period. Then put a sheet over the tray so the pictures are not visible. Remove a picture and encourage the children to find out which picture is missing. Sing the song/rhyme related to the missing picture.

### Taking it forward

- Watch TV cooking programmes with signing included.

### Observation questions

- Can the child link sound to a letter or image?
- Is the child interested in signs/symbols? Does the child ask questions?

### What's in it for the children?

The game develops the children's capacity to observe and remember small details of pictures.

50 fantastic ideas for exploring food

# Gingerbread Man storyboard
Literacy

## What you need:

- Storybook of *The Gingerbread Man*
- A large cardboard box
- Soft cardboard boxes in various sizes
- Newspaper, magazines
- Paper
- Coloured pencils
- Scissors
- Glue
- Two-sided, self-adhesive Velcro tape
- Large piece of felt (optional)

## What to do:

1. To make the board: flatten a large cardboard box to create a board, then trim the edges. Depending on the space given, it can be free standing or hanging. For a free standing board cut two large triangles out of a serrated, strong cardboard with a knife, mark and bend lengthwise and glue to the bottom on the back of the board. Optionally, cover with felt fabric for a nicer finish, however this is not necessary.

2. Cut Velcro tape in small, 2 cm pieces and secure one side onto the board, in random positions.

3. Listen to *The Gingerbread Man* story together.

4. Create small story characters and objects for all those mentioned in the story by drawing or cutting them out from newspaper/magazines. Glue them on cardboard, then cut around them and finally apply other piece of Velcro tape on the back.

5. Ask children to act out the story of *The Gingerbread Man*, by sticking their own characters onto the storyboard and moving them about.

## Taking it forward

- Make a storyboard for the *Little Red Hen* story.
- Ask children to create their own cooking related stories and act them out on a storyboard

## Observation questions

- Does the child show an interest in storytelling?
- What is the child's vocabulary like?
- Can the child remember short sentences?

## What's in it for the children?

Children will start to handle print with personal interest. They will be be able to repeat simple storylines back to you.

# Food shopping around the world

## What you need:

- Internet connection
- Printer and paper

## What to do:

1. Work with the children to do an internet search finding images of shopping bags and food stores around the world. Download food shop leaflets.

2. Print images of shopping bags and shop leaflets.

3. Use it to illustrate discussions about:
   - different food items
   - various advertising images
   - range of texts/languages.

### Taking it forward

- Collect a range of shopping bags and use them in role play.
- Design your own shopping bags.

### Observation questions

- Does the child understand how information can be retrieved from books/internet?
- Does the child show interest in images that carry meaning?

### What's in it for the children?

The activity develops the children's ability to observe and recognise details, similarities and differences, to find certain letters in print. It will develop children's sensitivity to foreign languages and foreign cultures and customs.

# Letter pretzels

Literacy

## What you need:

- Pretzel ingredients
  - 315ml warm water
  - 2 tsp instant yeast
  - 650g bread flour
  - 1 tbsp sugar
  - 1 tbsp salt
- Large mixing bowl
- Whisk
- Spoon
- Coarse salt
- 1 egg
- Lined baking tray
- Wire cooling rack

## What to do:

1. Make some pretzel dough: whisk flour, yeast, sugar and salt together. Add warm water. Stir together. Knead the mixture on a floured surface.

2. Divide the dough into equal portions (about 15) and shape it into a selection of letters with the children.

3. Place the shapes on a parchment-lined baking sheet.

4. Apply an egg wash (beat an egg and some water together) and sprinkle with coarse salt. Bake for 15-20 minutes until they are golden brown. Cool slightly on wire rack.

5. Play games while consuming your pretzels, for example finding the pretzel letter in their favourite storybook.

## Taking it forward

- Make children's initials.
- Make a sentence from letter pretzels.

## Observation questions

- Can the child recognise letters?
- Can the child link sounds to letters?

## What's in it for the children?

The activity develops the children's ability to observe and recognise the details, similarities and differences of letters in print (and pretzel!).

# Sensory kitchen

Expressive arts and design

## What you need:

- Dry ingredients
  - flour
  - sugar
  - salt
  - rice
- Scented ingredients
  - **spices** (cinnamon, cloves, mixed spice)
  - **herbs** (mint, parsley, coriander, dill)
- Liquid ingredients
  - honey
  - vinegar
  - golden syrup
  - lemon juice

## What to do:

1. Display the range of ingredients in bowls and on trays.

2. Encourage the children to touch, smell, taste and look at the ingredients while talking about the qualities of the items:

   - Let the children smell foods and describe the aroma. Does it smell like any other foods that they eat?

   - Let the children look at foods and describe the colour, shape, and size.

   - Ask children to listen as they eat food. Does the food make a sound? What is it?

   - Allow children to touch and manipulate foods. How does it feel? Is it squishy? Is it hard?

   - Encourage children to describe the taste, not just say if it tastes 'good', and to compare tastes. Is it sweet or sour? Does the grapefruit taste like a grape?

### Taking it forward

- Prepare sensory dishes such as herb salad with cider vinegar, fruit salad with maple syrup, bitter rocket and egg sandwich.

- Create an indoor herb garden.

### Observation questions

- Can the child recognise letters?

- Can the child link sounds to letters?

### What's in it for the children?

The activity develops the children's ability to observe and recognise details, similarities and differences, and to describe such characteristics in detail. It will encourage children to explore and discover through a variety of different media, such as food.

# Potion making for magic yoghurt

Expressive arts and design

## What you need:

- Fresh or dried edible flowers or flower oils such as rose, lavender, apple blossom, chive flower, cornflower, hibiscus, jasmine, marigold, nasturtium, rosemary flowers, tulip, viola etc
- Small bowl
- Taste and fragrance-free vegetable oil
- Pestle and mortar
- Small sieves (or tea strainer)
- Natural yoghurt

## What to do:

1. Introduce the different flowers to the children.

2. Observe the flowers by smelling and looking at them. Discuss the experience with the children and ask them to pick their favourites.

3. To extract the oils, place the children's preferred flowers into the mortar, crush vigorously and strain the oils produced.

4. Alternatively, add flowers to vegetable oils and allow them to impart their fragrance and flavour for unique, personalised floral oils.

5. Add to salads or natural yoghurt.

**Taking it forward**

- Make floral vinegar.
- Make floral tea.
- Decorate a cake or pudding.

**Observation questions**

- Does the child select appropriate resources and adapt work where necessary?

**What's in it for the children?**

The activity allows children to manipulate materials to achieve a planned effect, using a variety of resources with simple tools competently and appropriately.

# Bread sculpting

Expressive arts and design

## What you need:

- Measuring spoons
- Butter knife or wooden stick
- Plastic placemat or other smooth working surface
- Small ziplock storage bag
- Small, smooth glass or plastic bowl
- Three slices of stale white loaf bread
- Three tbs PVA white glue
- Three drops glycerin

### Health & Safety

Monitor children closely to ensure they don't nibble at the gluey dough.

## What to do:

1. To make bread-sculpting dough: remove and discard the crust from stale bread, reserving the white part. Crumble the bread into fine pieces in a bowl, add glue and mix until it forms a soft lumpy ball. The mixture will be sticky. Scrape and use everything left on the bowl sides. Pour out onto a clean work surface and allow to rest for about three minutes to dry a little. Pick a ball of dough up in your hands and knead it vigorously. Place in a ziplock bag for storage as this bread dough acts as an air drying clay, so work with small portions at a time.

2. Sculpt projects by rolling, cutting shapes and hand moulding. Glue pieces together if needed. Coat the finished sculptures using an equal mixture of glue and water. Allow to air dry for about a week. Coat again with the thinned glue mixture and leave until completely hard and dry. Soft bread dough keeps for up to three weeks if kept airtight and refrigerated. Finished sculpture pieces will last for years if encased or stored carefully, and kept away from moisture.

**Taking it forward**

- Use fresh bread dough to sculpt and bake edible sculptures.

- Colour the bread dough to create a different effect.

**Observational questions**

- Does the child use a variety of media to express their thoughts?

- Does the child show pride in their work?

**What's in it for the children?**

The activity allows children to freely express via the medium of bread dough. It also reinforces the message of sustainability by reusing food items that are not suitable for consumption.

# Taste test: juice making

## Expressive arts and design

## What you need:

- Green power juice ingredients
  - celery
  - cucumber
  - broccoli
  - pear
  - mango
  - lime
  - ice
- Red rebel juice ingredients
  - carrots
  - pear
  - orange
  - ice

Cheeky chops juice ingredients
  - mango
  - pineapple
  - kale

- Condiments and flavourings
  - honey
  - cinnamon
  - maple syrup
  - vanilla extract
  - salt
  - pepper
  - vinegar
- Juicer or food processor with sieve

## What to do:

1. Introduce all the ingredients to the children.

2. Observe the fruit and vegetables by smelling and looking at them. Discuss the experience with children and ask them to pick their favourites.

3. Peel and chop all the ingredients. Ask children to taste them and describe the flavour, and suggest what flavours would go together.

4. To make juices use:

   **Green power**
   ½ celery stick, 1 thick slice of cucumber, 1 small broccoli stem, 2 pears, ½ mango, 1 lime peeled, ice

   **Red rebel**
   2 carrots, 1 pear, 1 orange, ice

   **Cheeky chops**
   ½ pineapple, 4 kale leaves, 1 mango, ice

5. Allow children to create their own flavour combinations, emphasising that they have to choose both fruit and vegetable to go into their juice.

6. Put all items into a juicer, and process them. In the absence of a juicer, use a food processor or liquidiser and sieve.

7. Consume with ice.

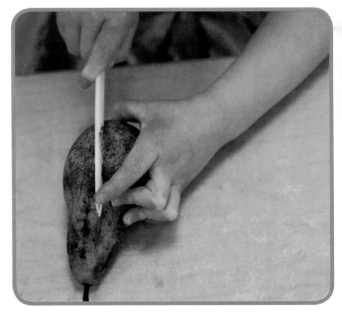

### Taking it forward
- Design labels for juice concoctions.

### Observation questions
- Does the child make their own choices?
- Does the child present original ideas?

### What's in it for the children?
The activity will help the children understand that different ingredients can be combined to create new effects.

# Texture cards
## Expressive arts and design

## What you need:

- Seeds
  - linseed
  - poppy seed
  - nigella seeds
  - pumpkin seed
  - sunflower seed
- Rice, lentils, beans
- Sugar, salt
- **Flour** (different types such as wheat, wholemeal, corn)
- Dried herbs
- Loose tea
- Transparent craft glue
- Glue stick
- Pieces of white, coloured card or cardboard

## What to do:

1. Introduce all the ingredients to the children.

2. Observe the items by touching, smelling and looking at them. Discuss the experience with the children and ask them to pick their favourites.

3. To make texture cards: cut pieces of card/cardboard for each child. Provide glue and ask the children to cover the surface thinly, spreading throughout. Sprinkle the children's chosen ingredient(s) all over the surface. Allow to dry completely.

4. Write words on the back of the cards such as bumpy, rough, smooth, scratchy, soft etc.

5. Play matching games, such as pulling out a card and finding matching surfaces in the environment, on own body etc.

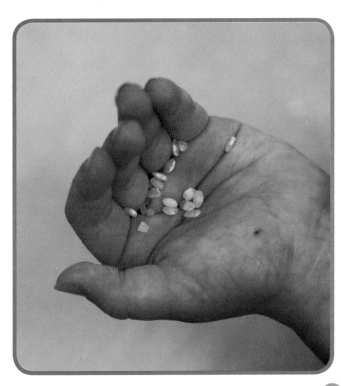

**Taking it forward**

- Make colour cards. For example: stick wheat, almonds, buckwheat on brown card, cover with paprika, lentils for red card, stick sugar, rice, flour on white card etc.

**Observation questions**

- Does the child happily experiment?

- Does the child understand simple representations such as certain objects represent smooth, certain objects stand for rough etc.?

**What's in it for the children?**

The activity enables the child to experiment in order to create new textures.

# Make your own apron

## Expressive arts and design

## What you need:

- Plastic bag
- Scissors
- Tape
- **Ribbons** (long enough to fit the waist and neck)
- Glue
- Embellishments such as beads, glitter, coloured tissue etc.
- Coloured markers

## What to do:

1. Cut the bag's sides, leaving the base intact, so that the apron's length can be adjusted according to the height required.

2. Measure the length and cut the base at the level needed.

3. Cut the sleeves and the neck according to preferences.

4. Take a ribbon bigger than the waist and after reversing the bag (so it will be on the inside of the apron when ready), tape the ribbon to it to create a fixed a strap. It can be done as two short bits of ribbon taped to the side of the apron only or as one long piece taped all over the breadth to make it sturdier.

5. Tape a ribbon to both the ends of the bag's handle, making sure that the whole loop passes through the head of the wearer.

6. Decorate the apron with markers, embellishments.

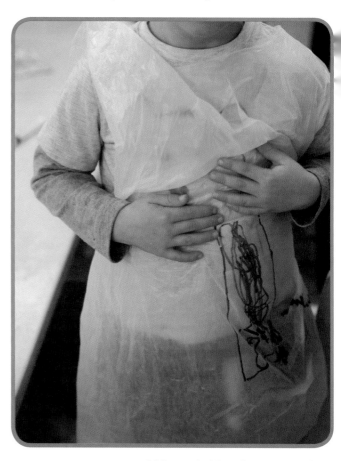

### Taking it forward

- Make a chef's hats from newspaper.

### Observation questions

- What materials does the child use?
- Does the child show preference when using different types of media?

### What's in it for the children?

Through trying different forms of expression, children can develop a preference for their favoured media. Children can learn about the sustainable nature of upcycling.

# Kitchen utensil musical

Expressive arts and design

## What you need:

- Wooden spoons
- Metal spoons
- Tongs
- Jugs
- Metal whisk
- Dried baking beans in a jar
- Metal bowls
- Metal lids
- Metal colander
- Forks
- Baking tins
- Pots and pans
- Music CDs

## What to do:

1. Provide the children with a selection of kitchen utensils.

2. Ask them to pick their favourites, then with a demonstration encourage them to imagine what sounds they can make.

3. Ask them to beat on a pan with a wooden spoon very softly for a quiet sound, then tell them to play harder and ask which sound was louder.

4. They can also imitate playing instruments like a piano, playing gently for a quiet sound or pressing harder for a louder sound.

5. Play music in the background to encourage the creation of rhythm.

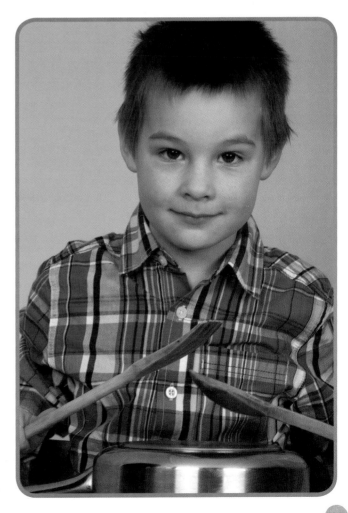

### Taking it forward

- Hang utensils on a string outdoors to create different sound effects.

### Observation questions

- Does the child move when hearing music?

- Does the child create simple rhythms?

### What's in it for the children?

Sound comparison activities provide opportunities for children to practise being loud or quiet. Children can explore ideas about rhythm, sound and movement while representing their own ideas and valuing their own discoveries.

50 fantastic ideas for exploring food

# Farm journey

Understanding the world

## What you need:

- Soil
- Builder trays or large shallow trays
- Toy or real vegetables
- Toy or real fruit
- Small rake, shovel
- Leaves
- Sticks (preferably collected by the children)
- Plastic animals
- Hay
- Corn
- Four chairs
- Black bin bag or sheet
- Rubber bands, clothes pins
- Fabric pieces or dressing up clothes
- Cardboard box
- Buckets
- Farm-themed books

## What to do:

1. Make a farm house by building a simple indoor den. Find a spacious corner. Position four chairs in a circle, getting just the right distances apart to make a good size den, without the roof collapsing. Use safety pins, elastics, pegs or paper clip clamps to connect sheets/bin bags together to keep them from falling down. Using rubber bands to tie blankets to chairs is also a good way to keep them suspended where you want them. Drape the sheets and blankets over the top of the chairs. Use rubber bands or clothes pegs to keep the blankets on. Create a door.

2. Position trays to create the animal areas: a pen, a coop, a sty. Fill them with hay and place plastic or soft toy animals on top.

3. Position trays in another are to create the growing fields. Place soil in them and spread vegetables.

4. Create a fruit orchard by placing leaves, sticks and fruit on a tray.

5. Draw a tractor on a cardboard box.

6. Provide a range of farm-themed books and encourage the children to dress up and role play, while talking about how our food comes from farms.

### Taking it forward

- Visit a real local farm or orchard.
- Organise a fruit picking trip.
- Set up a farm shop role play.

### Observation questions

- Does the child talk about some of the things they have observed such as plants, animals, natural and found objects?
- Does the child talk about why things happen and how things work?

### What's in it for the children?

Children can develop an understanding of growth, decay and changes over time, care and concern for living things and the environment.

# Cookie swap party

## What you need:

- Basic biscuit ingredients
  - 320-330g flour
  - 250g butter
  - 140g sugar
  - 1 egg
- Extra ingredients
  - raisins
  - chocolate chips
  - dried cherries
  - oranges
  - lavender oil
  - flowers
- Large mixing bowl
- Spoon
- Sieve
- Rolling pin
- Knife
- Baking sheet
- Wire cooling rack

## What to do:

1. Hold a cookie swap party, a German tradition.

2. To make basic dough: mix the softened butter and caster sugar in a large bowl with a wooden spoon, then add the egg yolk and 2 tsp vanilla extract and briefly beat to combine. Sift over 300g plain flour and stir until the mixture is well combined.

3. To make orange sticks: heat the oven to 180°C. Make the basic biscuit dough, adding the zest of two oranges to the sugar and butter mixture. After chilling, roll out the dough into a rough rectangle, then use a knife to divide the dough into long strips. Put in the oven and bake for 12–14 minutes. For the icing, mix 140g sifted icing sugar with 4–5 tbsp orange juice and the zest of an orange. When biscuits are cool, half dip them into the icing, then dry on a rack.

4. To make chocolate and fruit biscuits: heat the oven to 180°C. Make a batch of basic biscuit dough, substituting 50g cocoa powder for 50g of the plain flour. Add 85g raisins and 85g dried cherries, then mix well. Scoop the mixture into 12 large balls onto a non-stick baking sheet. Space well apart, as they will spread. Flatten slightly, bake for 12-15 minutes, then transfer the soft, warm cookies to a cooling rack to firm up.

5. To make lavender rounds: Prepare the basic biscuit dough, adding 2 tsp lavender extract, then roll in some finely chopped lavender flowers. Shape the dough into a large oval log, carefully wrap in cling film, then chill or freeze. To cook, heat oven to 180° C, then slice off 1cm thick ovals. Bake on a non-stick baking tray for 12 minutes until pale gold, then transfer to a cooling rack to firm up.

6. Make different varieties of cookies with small groups and encourage children to swap, tasting them all.

## Taking it forward

- Organise a cookie swap of biscuits made with parental involvement at home.

## Observation questions

- Is the child cooperating? Is the child ready to share information?

- Is the child talking about things they have seen or experienced?

## What's in it for the children?

Children can learn about different origins, occupations and ways of life. Children can develop an understanding of some of the things that make them unique, and can talk about some of the similarities and differences in relation to friends or family.

# Bread from different cultures

## Understanding the world

## What you need:

- French baguette ingredients
    - 380g flour
    - ¼ teaspoon instant yeast
    - 1 teaspoon salt
    - 230-300ml water

- Spanish King Cake/La Rosca de Reyes ingredients

    **Dry ingredients**
    - 450g strong white bread flour
    - 75g caster sugar
    - 7g instant yeast
    - ½ teaspoon salt

    **Wet ingredients**
    - 75g softened butter
    - 2 large eggs
    - 150ml milk
    - zest of 2 lemons
    - zest of 2 clementines
    - zest of 2 small oranges
    - 100g candied fruits

    **Glaze**
    - 75g icing sugar
    - 75g softened butter
    - 100g plain white flour
    - 1-2 tablespoons orange flower blossom water to mix

- Lussekatter/Swedish St Lucy Day Cardamom Bun ingredients

    - 300ml milk
    - 1 teaspoon saffron threads
    - 500g strong white flour
    - 7g fast-action dried yeast
    - ½ teaspoon salt
    - 100g caster sugar
    - 1 tsp cardamom pods
    - saffron threads
    - 75g butter
    - 1 large egg
    - 1 small egg
    - raisins

- Large mixing bowls

- Spoons

- Foil

- Oiled baguette tin

- Baking sheets

## What to do:

1. Organise themed days to try the different traditional breads.

2. To make the baguette: in a large bowl combine all the ingredients to create a wet dough. Cover with foil and let it rest for about 20 hours. Knock back (knead or punch down) and shape by placing in an oiled baguette tin (alternatively leave as two long strips). Let it rise for a further two hours. Bake in a 200-220° C oven for about 45 minutes or until golden brown and crisp.

3. To make King Cake: mix the dried ingredients and then add the rest of the ingredients and knead by hand for about ten to 15 minutes. Allow to prove overnight. Take the dough out of the bowl and cut into three even sized pieces; roll them into balls and then roll them into long sausage shapes. Lay them on the floured board and plait them, before making a ring and joining them together with a little flour and water. Place on a baking tray. Mix the butter, icing sugar, flour and the orange flower water to make a stiff paste. Decorate the ring and place candied fruit on top. Cover and allow to prove for 1 hour, or until the ring has nearly doubled in size. Bake in a pre-heated oven 180° C for 30 to 40 minutes; the cake is ready when it is golden brown, well risen, and sounds

hollow when tapped underneath.

**4.** To make St Lucy buns: butter a large baking sheet. Soak the saffron threads in the milk. Combine the flour, yeast, salt, sugar and cardamom in a large bowl and then make a well in the centre and add the saffron milk, beaten large egg and melted butter. Bring it all together like bread dough, turn it out onto a floured board and knead for ten to 15 minutes until smooth and elastic. Let it prove in a warm place for about an hour, until it has doubled in size. Pre-heat oven to 200° C. Place the dough on a floured board, knead and divide it into 12 equal sized pieces. Take each piece in turn and roll it out into a long strip, before twisting it into an 'S' shape very tightly. Place the shaped buns onto the prepared baking sheet and allow them to rise for 45 minutes in a warm place. Brush the tops with a beaten egg and then push a raisin into the centre of each scroll. Bake them for 15 to 20 minutes in a pre-heated oven until they are dark golden brown and sound hollow when tapped underneath.

## Taking it forward

- Make breads for harvest festival.

- Use the internet to research different shapes of bread from different cultures.

- Ask children to design their own family bread.

## Observation questions

- Does the child talk about some events from their own lives?

- Does the child recognise any special times?

## What's in it for the children?

Children can learn about the lives of people, remember and talk about significant events in their own experience, show interest in other cultures, and describe special times or events.

# Spices around the world

## Understanding the world

### What you need:

- Large white card
- Marker
- A world map
- Glue
- Internet connection
- A large variety of spices

### What to do:

1. During this activity the children will smell and study various spices and research their country of origin. After drawing a map they will glue samples of each spice on its country of origin to create a tactile map for using in cooking activities.

2. Draw/copy a true-to-life map. Add additional small details such as rivers, lakes, islands or larger towns. Colour and decorate.

3. Search on the internet to gather information about different spices and where they originate.

4. Help the children glue small samples of each spice onto its country of origin.

5. Gather information or ask the children to imagine how the spices can be used in cooking.

### Taking it forward

- Encourage the children to create fantasy maps from their imagination or based on classic stories e.g. 'Where did Little Red Riding Hood take grandmother's cake?' or 'Where is Snow White's apple orchard?'.

- Make a tea-map.

- Make small portions of bread pudding with different spices (see recipe on page 61).

### What's in it for the children?

Children can learn about different cultures while talking about foreign countries. Making a world map will strengthen the children's ability to pay attention to detail.

# Harvest around the world

Understanding the world

## What you need:

- White card
- Glue
- Straw
- Scissors
- Tape
- Thanksgiving sandwich
  - sliced turkey
  - sweetcorn
  - roast pumpkin
- Bread pudding ingredients
  - 100g sugar
  - 1 teaspoon ground cinnamon
  - 5 slices of any bread
  - butter
  - 2 apples, peeled and chopped
  - dried berries
  - raisins
  - 350ml milk
  - 2 eggs

## What to do:

1. **Polish harvest:** make simple paper crowns decorated with straw to celebrate Polish harvest. In Poland at the end of harvest (which is traditionally on or around 15th August) a crown of straw was placed on the head of a village girl. The mayor of the village then placed a rooster on top of the crown. The girl led the way from the fields with musicians and villagers. It is said that if the rooster crowed it was considered lucky and the future would be good.

2. **American harvest:** eat a traditional dish to celebrate the American Harvest (Thanksgiving) which is honoured on the fourth Thursday in November, to celebrate the first harvest of the English settlers in America nearly 400 years ago. The first puritan settlers, known as the Pilgrim Fathers, were the founders of their nation. The festival is celebrated with a special family meal, consisting of turkey, sweet potato, sweetcorn and cranberry sauce, followed by sweet pumpkin pie for dessert.

3. **English harvest:** use the great autumn produce in a bread pudding to celebrate the English harvest. Preheat the oven to 190° C. Lightly grease a baking dish. Mix together the sugar and cinnamon. Butter five slices of bread and cut in half. Layer the bread in the dish, adding a handful of chopped apples, raisins and the sugar. Mix the milk and eggs together and whisk. Pour over the bread and leave to absorb for ten minutes. Bake in the oven for 35 to 45 minutes, until the pudding is set and browned.

**Taking it forward**

- Make a harvest fruit juice from apples and grapes.

**Observation questions**

- Does the child make comments?
- Does the child ask questions?

**What's in it for the children?**

Children can learn about history and traditions.

# foraging trip

Understanding the world

## What you need:

- Waterproof clothing for children
- Small knives
- Small baskets/ trugs/plastic bags
- Hand towels
- Water bottles
- Field guides
- Apple sauce ingredients
  - 225g cooking apples peeled, cored and chopped
  - zest of a lemon
  - 2 tbsp water
  - 15g butter
  - 1 tsp sugar
  - 1 tsp honey
  - a handful of fresh blackberries, chopped
- Books about plants

## What to do:

1. Look for field guides to edible plants at your local library; connect with an advanced wild food enthusiast; find a foraging mentor through your local nature centre; discover a few favourite foraging sites nearby.

2. Check with your local park office to determine if foraging is allowed on their property.

3. Forage plants that are easy to pick and hard to confuse with anything else such as berries (blackberries, raspberries, strawberries, elderberries); dandelions, rosemary, lavender, ramson (be weary of its similarity to Lily of the Valley which is poisonous) or watercress.

4. To make apple sauce with blackberries: put all the ingredients listed in a saucepan. Cover and cook over a low heat until they are soft and mushy.

✚ **Health & Safety**

Obtain parental permission for field trips and ensure appropriate ratios of adults to children. Check for allergies.

## Taking it forward

■ Make the children's own foraging cookbook.

■ Make the children's own foraging map.

■ Cook with foraged ingredients: herb bread, berry jam, wild garlic soup etc.

## Observation questions

■ Does the child show interest in their environment?

## What's in it for the children?

Children will become calm in the quiet natural areas and they will develop an ability to focus on nature. It helps children to better understand the earth, learning about habitat, wildlife, weather, microclimates, soil, and more.

# Video-recipe: cupcakes

## Understanding the world

## What you need:

- Sponge cake ingredients
  - 125g butter
  - 125g self-raising flour
  - 2 eggs
  - 125g caster sugar
  - 2 tsp vanilla extract
- A large bowl
- Sieve
- Metal spoon
- A muffin tin
- 12 cupcake cakes
- Icing sugar to decorate
- Wire cooling rack

**Taking it forward**

- Make a video advert for the children's restaurant.

**Observation questions**

- Can the child operate simple equipment? Is the child keen to use technology?
- Is the child excited to observe new technology?
- Does the child seek to acquire basic skills in technology (to turn on or off the equipment)?

**What's in it for the children?**

Children will learn about technology. They will be able to anticipate repeated sounds, sights and actions, for example when an adult demonstrates actions several times. They will show interest in objects, tools with buttons, flaps and simple mechanisms, and begin to learn to operate them.

## What to do:

**1.** Before videoing:

  - Pick a recipe.
  - Choose a location, organise the background.
  - Prepare required ingredients and necessary tools.
  - Set the camera up.
  - Choose and play music in the background (check copyright).
  - Choose the presenters, organisers, film directors,

**2.** To make the sponge cake: heat the oven to 180° C. Line the muffin tin with cupcake cases. Cream the butter and the sugar together until pale. Beat in the eggs and vanilla extract. Sift over the flour and fold in using a large metal spoon. Add a little milk. Divide the mixture between the cupcake cases. Bake for 20-25 minutes until an inserted skewer comes out clean. Allow to stand for five minutes before putting on to a wire rack to cool.

**3.** Tips: make sure you capture a variety of wide shots and close-ups. Stand on top of the table to grab an aerial view, or get a low angle to show the pouring in of ingredients from the bowl's perspective. Hold your camera steady and make sure to get at least ten seconds of each section. Video the scenes in sequential order, from beginning to end. Don't stay on one shot for too long. Ask one of the children to introduce titles by voice over or by walking across with a sign.